This book is dedicated to my son

and to everyone else who ever

had a love for running around
chasing fireflys.

The boy in the book is my son and
the girl in the book is me. I hope
you will enjoy reading this book as
much as I enjoyed making it.
Love,
Adriane Currie

Oh Firefly!!
I Love You!

Oh Firefly!!

Illustrated by Adriane Currie

Author: Adriane Currie

Oh

Firefly !!

Author: Adriane Currie

Oh Firefly,

You twinkle in the sky

You fly up oh so high

Like a butterfly in the sky

Oh Firefly

You are delightful to my eyes

As you fly throughout the night,

With your green light flashing bright

Like an airplane in the night

Oh firefly,
you are like a magician
at night.

Disappearing before my eyes.

Just for a moment after you

blink so

BRIGHT!

Oh firefly,
You blink so
fast at
night. Like a buoy warning
on the water at
night.

Oh Firefly

Your twinkle is so bright

You light up all the night

Like a glowstick shining bright

Firefly!!

Please

Let

Catch

www.ingramcontent.com/pod-product-compliance
Lightning Source LLC
Chambersburg PA
CBHW060826290526
45792CB00005BB/1823